Take control of your attention — or others will.

Your attention is your property. When you take control of your daily experiences, you increase your success, satisfaction, and confidence.

You Know That Feeling

Where You've Been Rewarded

When Others Own Your Attention

How You Lose Attention

Getting It All Back

Courage Is Capability

Incredibly Fast Progress

Your 100% Keeps Expanding

Six Ways To Enjoy This Strategic Coach Book

Text **60 Minutes**	The length of our small books is based on the time in the air of a flight between Toronto and Chicago. Start reading as you take off and finish the book by the time you land. Just the right length for the 21st-century reader.
Cartoons **30 Minutes**	You can also gain a complete overview of the ideas in this book by looking at the cartoons and reading the captions. We find the cartoons have made our Strategic Coach concepts accessible to readers as young as eight years old.
Audio **120 Minutes**	The audio recording that accompanies this book is not just a recitation of the printed words but an in-depth commentary that expands each chapter's mindset into new dimensions. Download the audio at **strategiccoach.com/go/yayp**
Video **30 Minutes**	Our video interviews about the concepts in the book deepen your understanding of the mindsets. If you combine text, cartoons, audio, and video, your understanding of the ideas will be 10x greater than you would gain from reading only. Watch the videos at **strategiccoach.com/go/yayp**
Scorecard **10 Minutes**	Score your "Your Attention: Your Property" mindset at **strategiccoach.com/go/yayp**. First, score yourself on where you are now, and then fill in where you want to be a year from now.
ebook **1 Minute**	After absorbing the fundamental ideas of the "Your Attention: Your Property" concept, you can quickly and easily share them by sending the ebook version to as many other individuals as you desire. Direct them to **strategiccoach.com/go/yayp**

Thanks to the Creative Team:

Adam Morrison

Kerri Morrison

Hamish MacDonald

Shannon Waller

Jennifer Bhatthal

Suvi Siu

Christine Nishino

Willard Bond

Peggy Lam

Alex Varley

Your Attention: Your Property

Every day, there are multiple things vying for our attention—people, businesses, technologies, apps. But many of us don't realize that our attention is our property. It belongs to us just like any other resource we own. And when we choose what we give our attention to, we can focus fully on our own purpose and on what's best for us.

When you take a step back and think about your thinking, you can take control of your attention, as well as your time and your purpose, rather than allowing others to be in control. It's up to you.

Strategic Coach®, The Strategic Coach® Program, The Strategic Coach® Signature Program, Free Zone Frontier™, Unique Ability®, Self-Multiplying Company™, The D.O.S. Conversation®, The Self-Managing Company®, The Lifetime Extender®, Free Days™, Focus Days™, Buffer Days™, Unique Ability® Teamwork, The Largest Cheque®, and The 10x Ambition Program™ are trademarks of The Strategic Coach Inc.

Cartoons by Hamish MacDonald.

Printed in Toronto, Canada. The Strategic Coach Inc., 33 Fraser Avenue, Suite 201, Toronto, Ontario, M6K 3J9.

This publication is meant to strengthen your common sense, not to substitute for it. It is also not a substitute for the advice of your doctor, lawyer, accountant, or any of your advisors, personal or professional.

If you would like further information about The Strategic Coach® Program or other Strategic Coach® services and products, please telephone 416.531.7399 or 1.800.387.3206.

Library and Archives Canada Cataloguing in Publication

Title: Your attention : your property / Dan Sullivan.
Names: Sullivan, Dan, 1944- author.
Identifiers: Canadiana 20210279133 | ISBN 9781897239766 (softcover)
Subjects: LCSH: Attention.
Classification: LCC BF321 .S85 2021 | DDC 153.7/33—dc23

Contents

Introduction
Managing Your Own Attention
You're now taking full control of your attention and using your improved ability to focus for your own purposes.

I've been coaching entrepreneurs for decades, and one of the most significant impacts of our coaching program on our clients over long periods of time is that they get a handle on managing and directing their own attention toward what's most beneficial and useful for them.

At the same time, they develop an immunity to having their attention pulled away from them by other people or situations. (And there's never a lack of people trying to control where you put your attention!)

The game for everyone involved in the marketing and advertising world is to grab other people's attention and use it for their own purposes. Of course, at Strategic Coach, we want to get people's attention too, but what we offer is improved attention management and a greater ability to think about your own life in a way that leads to greater happiness through the use of our tools.

Being fully focused.
In the business world, the emphasis tends to be on time management. But time management isn't really the issue because that would mean you're relating to a measurement outside of yourself, something you can't control.

Attention management, on the other hand, is something you can control. It means you're aware of your own thinking and have a sense that you're totally in the present with yourself. You're very clear that you're focusing on something, and you're noticing that whatever you're focusing on has your full attention. You experience right away that there's a very different feeling and energy that comes when you're fully focusing your attention, and you get unique value from the way you personally manage your own attention.

They're after your attention.

Most people who are trying to capture your attention are only trying to sell you something. The only thing they care about is getting a certain number of people's attention on a particular product.

They don't care about making you a better, more focused person. They just want to use your attention for their own reasons, not because having your attention is of benefit to you.

But, like most people, you probably don't like being told what to do. The only situations in which you'll gladly give your attention to someone else are when doing so means you'll gain something useful from it. To put it another way, you'll let someone else have your attention if they're going to use your attention for your purposes, not for their own.

You might be able to distinguish between these situations by the kinds of questions you're being asked. If someone is asking you to pay attention to their experience, that's one thing, but if they're asking you to think about your own experiences, that's something else entirely.

Strengthening the right muscle.

You want to be focused on yourself as a unique individual and on how you're looking at your own life.

I think of doing this as using a particular muscle—one that a lot of people haven't used before. That's why they have a difficult time putting their focus on their own interests and why they're very easily pulled away to focus their attention toward somebody else's purpose.

But you can strengthen this muscle, and at Strategic Coach, we provide tools and concepts that help you do just that. We show entrepreneurs how they can gain greater and greater management and control over their attention so they can direct it toward whatever they choose.

At any time, you can start taking advantage of the lasting methods we've developed, which you can trust will always work. You can start thinking differently.

The more you practice this, the better you get at it, and there's no upper limit to how good you can get at focusing on your own interests. And once you gain management of your own attention, there's a natural movement on your part to help others focus on what's important to them.

You have the right.

I think entrepreneurs tend to manage their own attention better than most people, and this is partly what gives them the confidence to become entrepreneurs in the first place. A lot of people need to be employed because they can't focus their attention on money-making activities the way entrepreneurs can.

Entrepreneurs have developed the attitude that their attention is their property, and they manage their attention in the same way they manage other areas of their property.

People will say, "Do I have the right to do this?" And the answer is always that you have the right to do this if you say you have the right to do this. It's your attention, and you can decide right now to take complete ownership and control over it.

Thinking about your attention.

Focusing your attention is how you gain the ability to actually experience how you're thinking about things. I call this "thinking about your thinking." At any given time, you can step back and not only see what your attention is focused on, but experience how you're giving something attention and how you're fully conscious and present with the particular experience you're having.

This is not the case for people who are totally consumed by things outside of themselves. They have emotional reactions to physical things, to other people, and to other people's thoughts, but they themselves aren't having their own clear thoughts about what they're giving their attention to.

People like this will eventually have to react to something in a way that involves thinking about their thinking, and since this is a rare occurrence for them, and it usually happens in a negative situation, they can start to associate thinking about their thinking with negative situations.

But until you're thinking about your thinking, you can't direct your attention. And if you can't direct your attention, you're continuously reacting to unpredictable things that happen to you. When you think about your thinking, however, you're completely in control.

Chapter 1
You Know That Feeling

You have great memories of situations where you felt totally in control of your attention, and you know those were moments when you were completely focused on your own unique purpose.

The moment you step back from having your attention taken up by other people and their thoughts, and you're fully engaged in what you're doing, it's an automatically energizing experience. That's because, for a period of time, you're not being controlled from the outside.

And you can get better at it. In any circumstances, you can ask yourself, "How am I thinking about my thinking in this situation?" All of a sudden, you'll get a settled, peaceful feeling about it.

Your greatest memories are probably of times when you had an energizing sense of thinking, deciding, and acting for your own unique reasons. When you feel that you're in control of what you pay attention to, you truly experience yourself as being energetically alive.

Moments you remember most.
The specific experiences you likely remember most are ones where you were fully attentive. These experiences leave a much more powerful record in our memory than situations in which we weren't paying attention, where we weren't conscious of being conscious about the experience.

These experiences—and they can be as short as a few minutes—are the rock solid proof in your mind that you're truly alive and that you're a unique individual.

The chance to think about your thinking is readily available, but it's no surprise that for some people, it doesn't happen often. There are so many things vying for our attention nowadays, and in the course of most people's lives, they aren't asked or prompted to think about their thinking.

But once you've made this breakthrough, you've freed yourself. You recognize your own point of view about, and experience of, a situation, and now you own the experience.

Controlling your daily attention.

Once you've had, and recognized, these "uniquely alive" experiences, you'll daydream about having more of them— far more of them in the future than you've had in the past. You might think that maybe you just need better time management skills, but actually, deep down, you know that what you really need is more control of your daily attention.

I'm 77 at the time of writing this book, and I have far more control of my daily attention now than I've ever had before—far more than even just ten years ago, in fact. I'm less reactive to things. I know how to think about my thinking, and at this point, most of my activities are ones that involve being attentive, controlling my attention, being conscious about my own experiences, and owning those experiences.

I have avenues of productive activity that are scheduled in advance. My days are organized and channeled into activities where I access my attention.

And my knowledge of ways to direct my attention are increasingly productive, not only for myself, but for others.

Focused on unique purposes.

On a planet with eight billion people, so much unpredictable "stuff" is happening that it's impossible for anyone to understand what everyone else is trying to accomplish.

But it's totally possible for you to increasingly focus and expand your daily attention on your own unique purposes.

Generally speaking, you don't need to worry about what other people are up to. Their activities don't detract from yours, and you don't have to pay attention to them.

But when it comes to your own attention, not only can you control and manage it, you're also developing the capability of enabling other people to do the same thing. So it's a double reward.

Being energetically alive.

When I find myself frustrated with something, I tell myself to just think about my thinking about it—and the frustration disappears. It happens immediately.

What this tells me is that frustration comes not from the situation itself, but from our own inability to fully pay attention to it.

For an example of how this works, you can focus on one of your own unique purposes right now, and do it for the next ten minutes. Focus on an achievable, important project that can be started and completed today. Then do it. It's guaranteed to make you feel energetically alive. And doing it again tomorrow will be easier.

Free from outside control.

Every time you repeat this energizing achievement, your control of your attention improves. Each time, you feel energetically stronger. And while you're focusing your attention on your own unique projects, for your own unique purposes, what's happening outside is other people's business.

Like all human beings, you're controlled by a lot of factors, such as the laws of gravity and temperature. But this realm of thinking about your thinking is one that's completely yours.

No one else's permission is required to do anything in the domain of your own attention and consciousness. You can do anything you want here, including getting better and better at controlling your attention and consciousness.

And the more you do it, the more it raises the value of your time. You prefer doing things in certain ways because those ways are what you've found to be the most conducive to having a useful experience. Also, you'll get increasingly good at recognizing when someone else is not fully paying attention to the experience and will therefore not be worth your time to engage with.

On the other hand, you'll recognize right away when you're engaging with someone who is also thinking about their thinking, and in these situations, you'll enhance each other's ability to be extremely attentive.

EVERYBODY LOVES...
ALIVE
ATTENTION
ATTENTION
NJOYA
FULL
FREE
WOW!
ATTENTION
ENJOYABLE
ALIVE
FULL
FREE
FULL
THIS IS AMAZING!
ATTENTION
ENJOYABLE
FULL
ALIVE
ATTENTION
ENERGIZING
FULL

Chapter 2
Where You've Been Rewarded
You can see that your biggest progress, achievement, and success have come from fully focusing your attention.

When we're fully attentive, we use our capabilities in the best possible way. At these times, we're at our most skillful, our most strategic, and our most useful.

And it isn't only the eventual success that leaves us feeling rewarded. It's also that being fully conscious and attentive while we do the work makes the activity extremely enjoyable.

Someone else might achieve the desired result because they're skillful enough, but if they aren't fully controlling their attention and applying it, they'll be bored with the activity and won't feel rewarded.

Think about the most rewarding experiences of your past, in any area of your life. When you've focused fully on making positive progress, you've always been rewarded.

You're a high achiever every single time you do this. All of your best success, in both your personal and work life, has always been the result of being completely in control of your attention, focused on getting a new, bigger, and better result.

You're most useful to others.
You know from your most memorable experiences that opportunities to be uniquely useful to others always focus your attention more than anything else does.

Whenever you do this, you feel enormously rewarded, regardless of whether you're acknowledged by those benefiting from your help. The activity itself is greatly rewarding.

Doing the activity is a personal experience, and you can count on that reward every time because it doesn't depend on anyone else's reactions. Nothing feels better than being uniquely useful to another person.

You value what your mind can do with your own experience, and when someone responds in the intended way to your being useful, it's a double reward because you get proof outside of yourself that the way you think, the way you imagine a solution, and the way you then provide that solution is useful and valuable.

Your skills expand.

Some people will be useful only up to a certain point because if they provide something of value to someone else, they always expect the other person to reciprocate — and they'll get angry about it if they don't. But in this situation, they're giving up control. They're being controlled by someone else's non-response, someone else's behavior.

I've adopted the attitude of, "I'm just going to be useful and useful and useful, and everything will work out."

And it does work out because anytime, and in any way, that you expand one of your skills, you feel immediately rewarded for the effort.

Feeling more skillful — even when it's the result of responding to difficult, dangerous, and unhappy situations — is always rewarding to you afterward because you had to be fully attentive.

When you don't fully engage, you don't enjoy the experience. But when you fully engage, you always enjoy the experience, and you always get rewarded.

You're clear and calm.

You feel especially rewarded for being attentive in situations where everyone around you is flustered, bothered, confused, and anxious—but you are clear and calm. Almost nothing feels better than keeping your head when everyone else seems to be losing theirs. It is deeply satisfying.

When you're fully attentive, your actions are economical. You don't do too much, and you don't do too little. You just do what's required by the situation. And that feeling you get from being efficient, doing what the situation requires and nothing more, is a wonderful reward.

You rightfully take pride in those occasions when you maintain proper thinking when other people can't think properly. Also, when you think quickly and clearly in a situation where others can't, that's a sign that you've got your act together.

You like yourself.

When you think of those experiences where you were fully attentive, you realize that the biggest reward in your business and personal life is liking who you are. You like who you've been so far, and you're looking forward to who you're going to be in your life ahead.

When someone is fully attentive, fully present, and fully conscious, there's nothing not to like about that person.

You've built this capability of paying attention, of being conscious, and of taking ownership of your experience, and that can give you a real sense of confidence about everything you might experience in your future.

Even a negative past experience can be seen as important and beneficial to who you are if you take ownership of it.

Your confidence grows.

Gaining greater control over your attention multiplies your confidence about the future.

Throughout your life so far, your ability to pay attention to what's most important to you has been tested in countless ways. Looking at your life from this perspective makes you feel increasingly rewarded for having passed these tests.

Who you truly are is what you are truly attentive to. In other words, when you have the ability to give something 100 percent attention, that's who you really are. And that can constantly expand.

It can also start at any moment, even for someone who has made a career of not paying attention. You'd have to put the work in to change long-term—or perhaps even lifetime—habits and develop new ones, and to strengthen those muscles. But you could reinvent yourself based on what you start paying your full attention to. The opportunity to do this is always available.

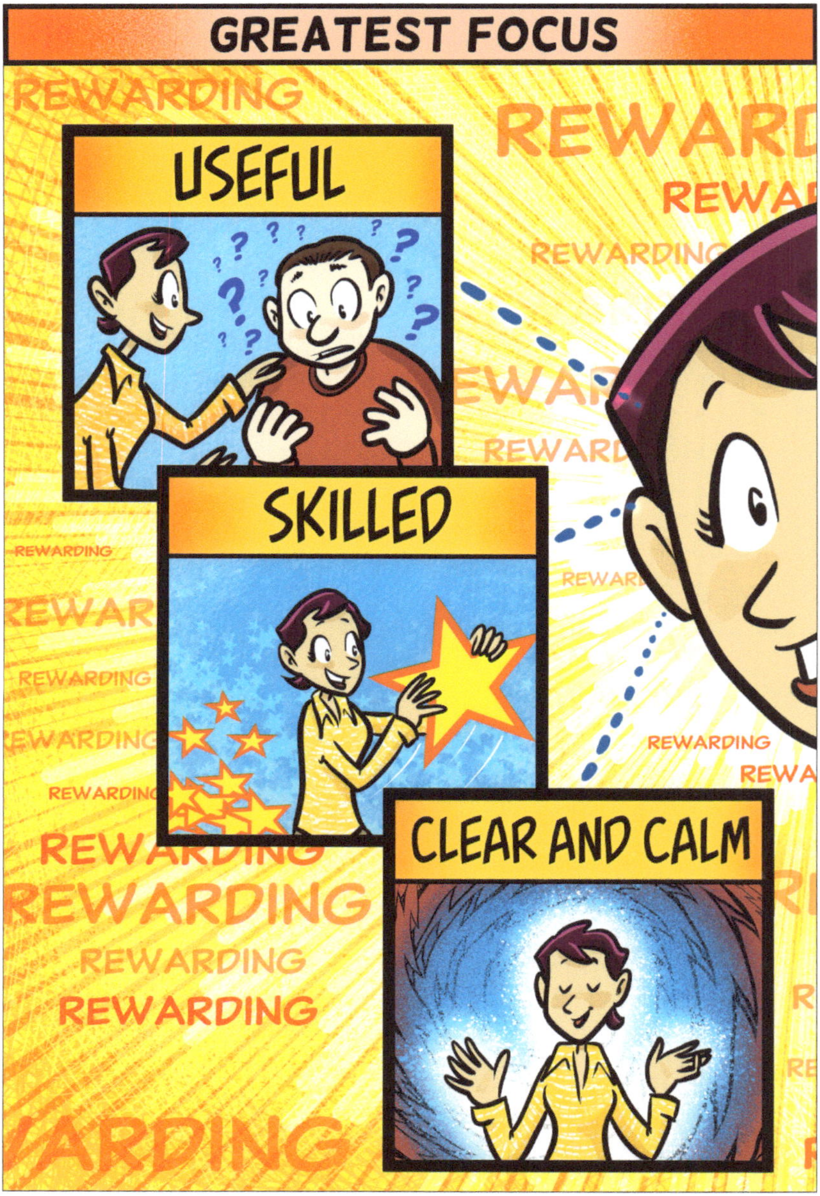
GREATEST FOCUS
USEFUL
SKILLED
CLEAR AND CALM
REWARDING

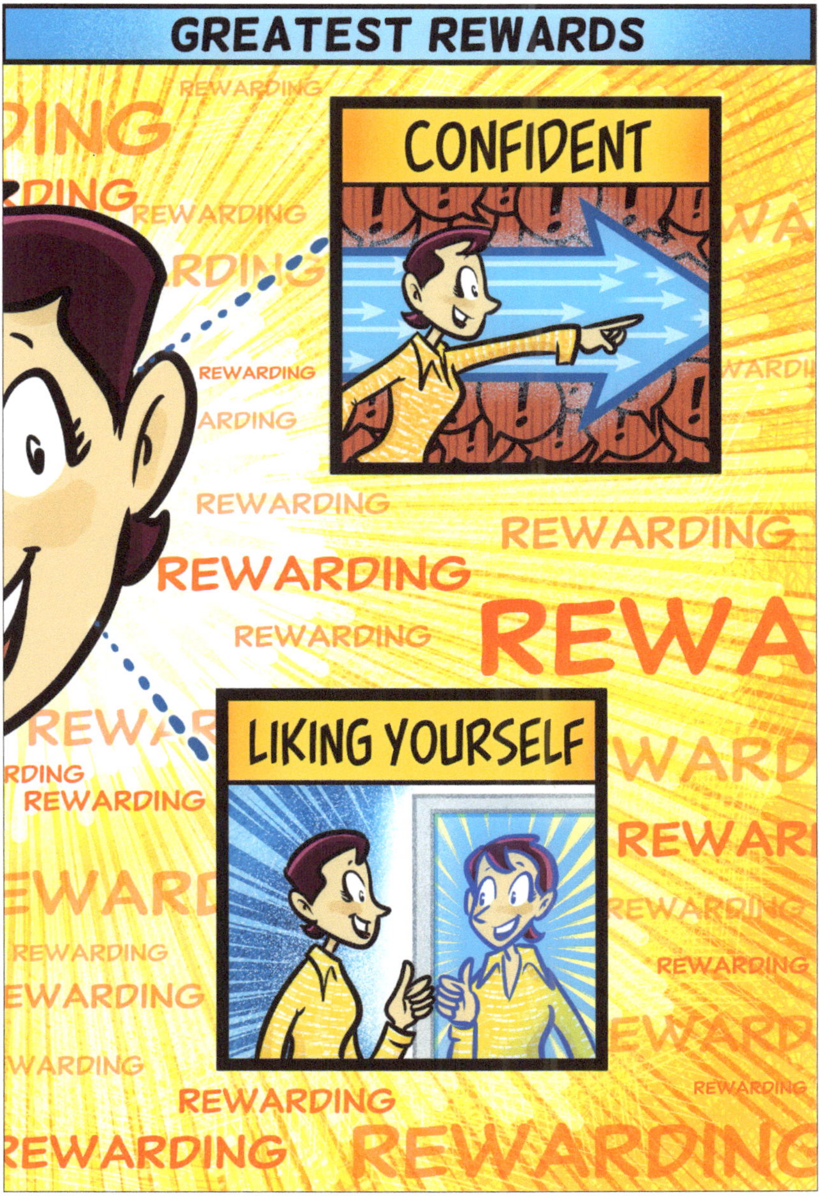
GREATEST REWARDS
CONFIDENT
LIKING YOURSELF
REWARDING

Chapter 3
When Others Own Your Attention
You realize that all of your anxieties and frustrations distract you when you allow others to control your attention.

You know that whenever you allow outside forces to own your attention, it bothers you. Some people try to attribute this feeling of being bothered to something outside of themselves, but it's you that's being bothered. You're giving your attention to something that isn't useful or rewarding.

Whatever the circumstances, however it's happening, you always feel a loss of energy, capability, and confidence when someone else controls your attention.

Now that you realize this, you can firmly commit to taking back increasing control of your daily attention. This can be difficult if you're used to someone else owning your attention—it might seem easier to let them have it. But you can build up the muscles required to keep your own attention if you work at it.

Bothered by being "owned."
You've been careless about staying connected to people who want to own part of your attention, especially through your computer and cell phone. You feel more and more bothered by these outside demands and distractions.

Generally, the people who are attempting to grab your attention don't really care about you. Facebook owns a lot of people's attention these days, but to them, it's purely transactional. They're trying to get a certain number of people to engage, and you're just a number in that scenario.

They're looking at quantity, not quality. They're using an algorithm to get your attention, and it can make you feel commoditized.

When your powerful attention has been used for something cheap and insignificant, you become less of who you are, and you feel that loss and diminishment. This can lead to having a life-long dislike of the people and companies who do this to you and those like them.

But when you control and use your full attention for your own purposes, the experience is transformational rather than transactional, and you become more of who you are.

Distracted and disrupted.

You can surely remember times in your past when you could focus for hours and even entire days on useful and enjoyable activities. You probably wish that it could be that way again, but it seems impossible to escape from constant disruptions.

At any time, there are any given number of things vying for your attention, making staying focused on what's important more and more of a challenge. Indeed, this is most people's experience most of the time.

But being able to focus on your enjoyable and useful activities is critical, especially for people who are committed to making a big impact on other people's lives by contributing valuable solutions. And it's critical to anyone for whom it's important to gain complete control of their own attention.

Lost energy and confidence.

Instead of your future looking bigger, it's looking more
bothersome. Instead of looking more dynamic and exciting,
it's looking more confusing and complicated, all of which is
causing you to worry.

And if things get bothersome, confusing, and complicated
enough, you won't feel like you have any sort of control at
all. And if you don't have any control at all, you may won-
der what the point is.

Right now, you imagine things only getting worse. When
you think about the future, you picture it as being hopeless,
and you're worried that you're not up to what that future
will require of you.

Fortunately, you suddenly remember crucial situations in
the past where you took a stand for yourself, where you
refused to be pushed around by outside circumstances.

Time to get angry.

You've done it before, and you know it's once again time to
get angry and make some decisive changes in how you're
approaching each day's experiences.

In the past, I've found myself in situations where I'm on
the wrong path. It could have been that I was pursuing
some activity that just wasn't going anywhere but I'd simply developed a habit of being there. And I had to get angry
to break the habit. I had to say, "That's it. I can't do this
anymore" and decide that what was happening simply
could not go on.

This can be any kind of situation, from an activity you're
in as part of a group to a hobby you spend time doing on

your own. The conscious part of your mind has to do an override on the unconscious part of your mind, and you need that strong emotion, that sense of anger. It's transformational anger.

Taking back control.

You're waking up to the fact that all your negativity is due to a single failure on your part: not treating your attention as your most valuable property. You've been letting other people use it for free, and every time you do this, you feel taken advantage of.

It's time to take back your control.

This is a binary thing. If you don't identify that everything that irritates you about your life right now is a function of something you're failing to do inside of yourself, you'll never come to grips with it. You'll continue looking at factors outside of yourself for what's bothering you.

So it's one way or the other. You're either going to try to control other people to prevent them from doing things that are bothering you, or you're going to correct what you're giving your attention to and recognize that allowing other people to control your attention is the real issue.

You can't control what other people are doing, but you can control what you're doing. Instead of fixating on factors you can't control, which will only get you down, you can get yourself into a space where you can take positive action.

OWNING YOURSELF
YOUR ATTENTION
LESSONS
YOUR PROPERTY
GROWTH
YOUR ATTENTION
YOUR PROPERTY
PROGRESS
SKILLS
TRANS-FORMATION
RESULTS
CREATIVITY
YOUR ATTENTION
YOUR ATTENTION
ENJOY-MENT
YOUR PROPERTY
CO-OPER-ATION
YOUR PROPERTY
REWARDS
YOUR ATTENTION

Chapter 4
How You Lose Attention
You realize that you lose control of your own attention when you think others' experiences are more important than yours.

You feel surrounded by and connected to many other individuals throughout your life, and if you haven't recognized and appreciated the unique value of your own experiences, it can seem that what other people think, say, and do is overwhelmingly important.

This makes sense because it takes a number of years after you're born before you develop the thinking ability to see yourself as a separate person, and in the meantime, you're getting lots of attention from other people who have more skills and knowledge than you have. It takes a while to reach the stage where you can talk to others and then decide for yourself what to do with the information you receive and whether that information is useful.

Some people continually lose ownership of their attention throughout their lives. But that's not you. Right now, you're suddenly waking up. You feel a great urgency to take back everything you've lost.

Dramatic discovery.
You're experiencing a dramatic discovery: you've been neglecting to manage and control your most important property.

Social media apps are always trying to capture your attention in order to make money. They'll claim it's okay because they're providing a free service, but that's not true. You're paying them with your attention, which is your most important property, and companies are relying on your not becoming aware that your attention is your property.

Anytime you give your attention away, you're letting someone else use your property without getting anything for it in return. You might think you're getting something in return when you're getting the use of something for free, but what you're doing is making your property—your attention—available for somebody else's purpose.

You can now recognize that you've been undermining your single most vital capability, and it might strike you as amazing that you haven't been aware of this before.

But now you are.

This means a dramatic change in your life. Now that you've grasped that your attention is your property, your thinking about what's best for your attention will go much deeper, and you'll be far more selective about what you give your attention to.

Surrounded by others.

For the first time, you comprehend the essence of the fundamental problem. For as long as you can remember, you've been surrounded by other individuals in every situation of your life, and you became convinced that their experiences were more important than your own.

This is because other people are better "packaged" than you feel. You're comparing their outsides with your insides, and it's unequal. You only see what they present to the world—you don't have access to their inner complexities. And so you make the judgment that they have it together more than you do and that their experience is more important than yours.

Theirs counts, yours doesn't.

It was always easier to focus on what others were doing and what they were saying about their experiences than it was to engage with and think deeply about what was happening to you.

But every time you discounted your own experience, you gave away your most important property.

The reason why it's easier to pay attention to others is because you only know the surface. When it comes to engaging with your own experiences, your emotions are involved, so you don't have the same clarity and objectivity that you do when looking at others' experiences.

Looking inward, you see all your complexities, but when you look at others' lives, it all seems so much simpler.

Suddenly waking up.

While you now recognize and accept that this is what's been happening in your life up until now, it doesn't have to be this way going forward.

You've suddenly realized what you've been doing and are now fully awake and committed to taking back control. As soon as you do this, you'll immediately find that it doesn't matter to you what other people think about, and you won't pay as much attention to their judgments or opinions.

At a certain point, you have to choose whether you're going to pay attention to what other people think is important or to what *you* think is important. And you have to be 100 percent all in with your choice.

Other people can give you information that might be useful, and you can take guidance from them, but you're the only authority on what your experience means.

Amazingly fast recovery.

Although you may not have been taking proper care of your most valuable property up until now, it's not too late to recover what you've lost. In fact, this realization can be amazingly energizing.

You can now be fully attentive to the problem because you already have the solution. What you pay attention to, and your ability to pay attention, is entirely your property, just like real estate you might own.

And the more you take it seriously as property, the less you'll find that your attention is being manipulated by other people, because you won't put up with other people using your property in a way that isn't good for you.

You're done with giving your attention to others and not getting anything out of it. You know now that this is a serious issue, with serious advantages for controlling your property and serious penalties for giving it away.

REGAINING ATTENTION

Chapter 5
Getting It All Back

You're relieved and happy that all of your lost attention starts coming back to you the moment you choose to take ownership of it.

You hadn't previously thought about your attention as your property, but now that you know it is, you don't want anyone misusing it, just as you wouldn't be happy if anyone took anything that belonged to you and used it up or returned it damaged.

And you know now that whenever you felt like you didn't have enough time, it was more likely that you didn't have enough attention.

But even though you may have gone years and decades without realizing that other people have "owned" your attention, you can now get it all back very quickly. The moment you make the decision, you can be fully attentive.

The difference you feel between being "owned" and being the "owner" is dramatically energizing. You'll begin with hours and then you'll have whole days of controlling and directing your full attention toward what you want to focus on, and outside distractions will lose their power to pull you away.

The moment you choose it.

Full attention comes back the very instant you recognize and claim it as your property. Before this realization, you may have felt distracted and powerless. But now you suddenly realize that you can be completely in control of what you pay attention to. It's simply a matter of choosing it.

And as soon as you choose to put your attention on something, that experience is your property too.

There's no point regretting past experiences in which others squandered your attention because even then you had the power to own your attention but you didn't know any better, so you gave it away. You surrendered it and got an experience that wasn't what you wanted. That's always the risk when you put other people in charge of your property.

From "owned" to "owner."
When you give up ownership of your attention, almost any bad thing you can think of might happen. All the negative experiences you've had in your life, the sense of frustration and failure that's piled up in your thinking for decades, was because you let other people and outside factors own your attention.

But now you feel your ownership. There's no reason anymore for you to feel resentful or as though you don't have enough time.

The times you allowed your attention to be owned by others weren't your fault. You didn't know then that your attention was your property and that you had a choice about what to use it on.

And just as that can't be held against you, you can't hold it against others who aren't owning their attention. You can only make them aware that they have a choice in the matter.

Distractions lose power.

Think of the countless times you resolved to improve yourself in different areas of your life. And each time you've done this, it was mostly so that you could gain the positive attention of other people—the ones who "owned" you! But all of these distractions are now gone.

Here's an example from my life. I grew up with a passion for watching sports, and that became locked in place. Then, at the age of 72, I realized that I was still devoting an enormous amount of time to it 50 years after it had actually been meaningful to me. That thought freed me. And still later, I realized that devoting my attention to television at all was not what I should be doing, so I stopped it entirely.

When you choose to devote your attention to big, worthwhile efforts, the contrast with frivolous things you could have chosen to spend your attention on becomes starker.

Dramatically energizing.

Before the sudden realization you're having right now about completely owning your attention, your daily experience may have been a struggle. It might have felt complicated, bothersome, and fatiguing. And tomorrow was going to be the same.

But with your full attention now back in your control, everything seems energizing.

This isn't gradual. At a certain point, there's a complete jump where you're suddenly on the other side of a previous way of operating, and now things are totally different. Your senses are sharper, your thoughts are more decisive, and you feel more energized.

I used to take naps during the day, and fall asleep on flights, but I don't feel the need to anymore. I get energized from the feeling that what I've been doing is important. And if you're owning your attention, everything's important—just as nothing is important when others control your attention.

Nothing's been lost.

All of the times in your life when you gave away your attention don't feel like a loss. Now that you understand that it's all about property, you feel totally forgiving and self-forgiving. You were just thinking about things in the wrong way.

But now you'll be thinking in the right way. Forever.

People have a tendency to judge themselves harshly, but just as you don't have the right to judge other people for what they did when they were younger, you don't have the right to judge your younger self for what you did before you became conscious that there was a better way. Not only that, but all the things you did when you were younger are valuable to you now.

You can now appreciate and value every part of your experience because you know it's all your property, and you want to treat it well. Now that you own your property and are taking complete responsibility for all your experiences, you'll see an abundance of opportunity all around you.

You've woken up, which means that nothing's going to be wasted, and all of what you see as your past failures can be transformed.

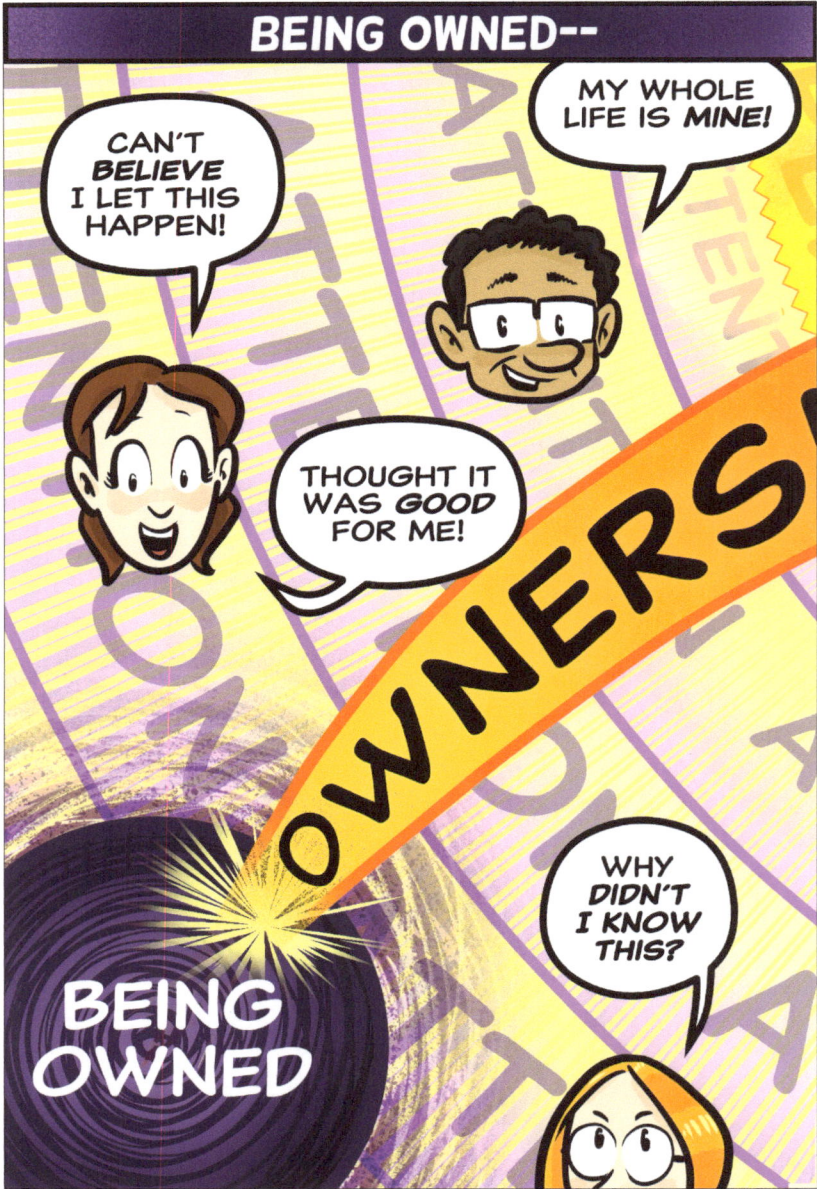

INSTANT ENERGY
NOBODY CAN STEAL FROM ME!
HIP
MY PROPERTY, MY FUTURE!
SO SIMPLE, SO SATISFYING!
THIS EXPLAINS EVERYTHING!

Chapter 6
Courage Is Capability
You are committed to taking back all of your attention — and your courage to do this provides 100% ownership.

You're already resolved to stop wasting your attention. From now on, you're committed to using your attention more and more for what *you* want, not for what others want.

This is a remarkably bold initiative in a disruptive world where so many others are constantly distracted. They give their attention away, and the more they do it, the harder it is for them to take their attention back. Part of the reason they do this is that they worry that not paying attention to what others are doing will leave them isolated, and they haven't yet developed a sense of self that's independent from other people.

Reclaiming your attention sets you apart, and you're resolved to go through with the experiment of being alone with your attention and whatever you choose to focus it on.

As soon as you decide to set out on this new path, you experience a dramatic difference. The courage of self-ownership is its own immediate reward.

Remarkably bold initiative.
You now know that your attention is the most valuable property you can ever possess. And this realization makes you resolved to reclaim your attention from all distractions that have crept into your daily life.

This doesn't mean there's anything wrong with having your mind engaged with other people, but there is a sense of uniqueness that comes from not worrying about what other people are doing and focusing your attention on your own activities and ideas.

Since it requires significant amounts of courage for someone to cut out distractions and stop giving away their attention to other people, the majority of individuals instead choose the path of cowardice. They carry on allowing others to own their attention, and they never gain the confidence to be by themselves, away from all distractions.

Meanwhile, using your courage to take that step means you're gaining 100 percent ownership of what's yours and that you're going to continually get better at controlling your attention.

Not the same person.

You're immediately aware that you're not the same person you were before becoming conscious of the importance of owning your attention. And you're astounded by all the ways you gave away your attention in the past. So many things that you once considered serious now seem silly.

Think about all the distractions that used to own so much of your attention. Now that you're aware of this and are resolved to getting all your attention back, consider just how much time and energy you wasted on those distractions and how many unnecessary complexities and complications they created in your life.

But there's no reason to feel embarrassed, stupid, or guilty about it. You can be calm and accepting, recognizing that what you used to do is the road that led you here—to controlling your attention and being free from those wasteful distractions.

Immediate difference.

Treating your attention as your property sets you apart from everyone else. Being different used to feel uncomfortable, even frightening, but now you feel calm about it. Before, it felt like a loss, but now it feels like a confident gain.

Being increasingly attentive is a win. The best kind.

What you experience in your life is unique to you. No one else is experiencing exactly what you're experiencing. In fact, your notion of who you are is the sum total of your experiences. And that's your property.

Reclaiming your attention as your property isn't as difficult as it would be to reclaim physical property that was in someone else's possession. When it comes to your attention, the moment you realize it's yours, you get all of it back.

Remember that everything you've experienced up until now, before you took back your attention, wasn't a waste of time. It was a learning process. And now that you're more conscious, you're aware of all the ways in which you weren't thinking consciously about your attention before.

Better than childhood.

Regaining your full attention is like starting your life over but with years of extraordinarily valuable experience. You feel young and energized again, but this time you have the unique knowledge and capability you've gained over the years.

It doesn't matter that it took a long time for you to own your attention. Nothing's been lost.

When you look back on troubling experiences you've had where you were trying and failing to find what you were looking for or to figure something out, you realize now that it was because you weren't consciously controlling your attention as you are now.

If you use your imagination, you can see how all of those painful experiences would have been quite different if your current self had been in those situations rather than your past self, knowing now what you didn't back then.

Courageous ownership.
You're gaining back your attention, and you're expanding your single most important property for your whole life. And you're doing it for one reason: you have the courage to break free from your distractions.

It's courageous because many people, even knowing the cost, will never own their life the way you're owning yours. It takes courage to experience life differently than the people around you. There's pressure to just go along with the way other people are doing things.

What you're doing is consciously rejecting systems that don't work for you. You're not okay with continuing to allow other people to benefit from using your attention—your most valuable property—while you don't benefit from it. You're taking your attention back, and you're going to get better and better at using it in ways that benefit you.

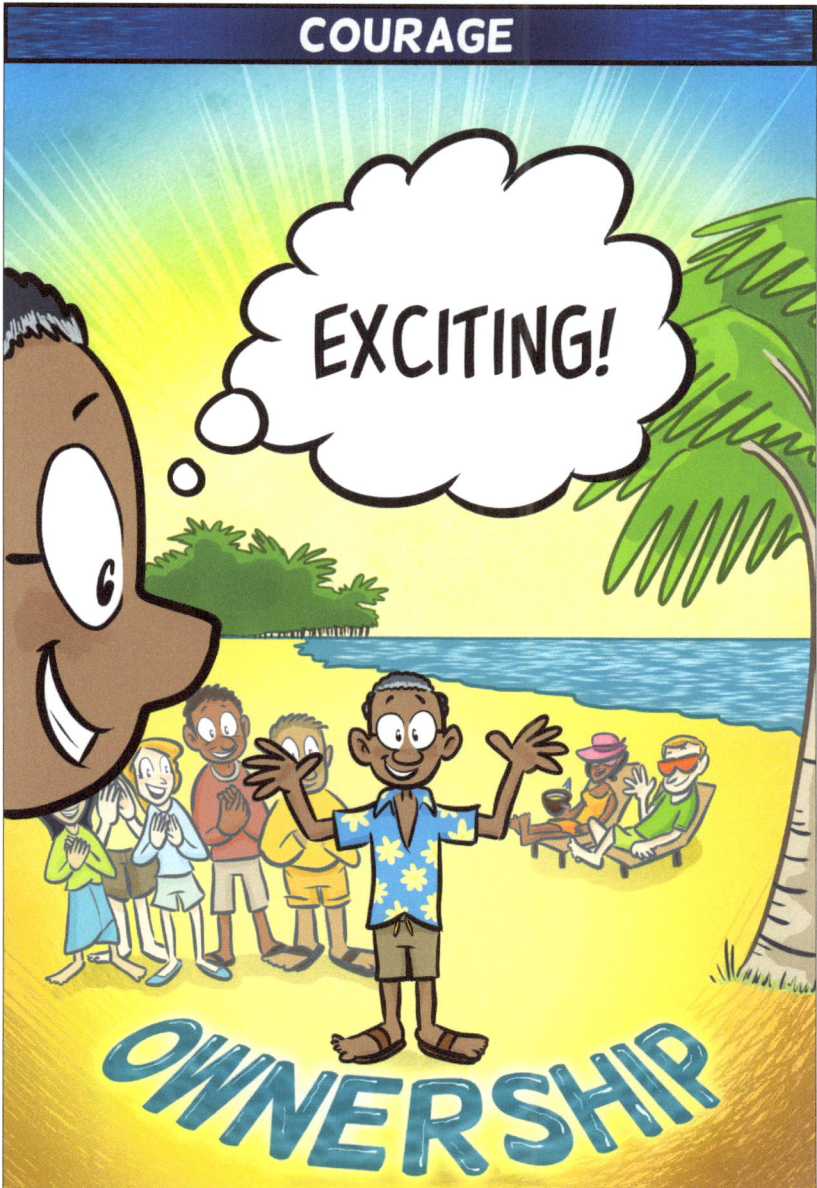

Chapter 7
Incredibly Fast Progress
You are amazed that decades of giving away your attention can be completely reversed in a remarkably short time.

The courage it took to take back control of your attention quickly transforms into an expanding capability. And this happens almost all at once. Today, you decided to regain your attention, you're already experiencing that difference, and soon you'll make amazing progress.

It's like flipping a light switch. It was completely off, and now it's completely on. And now all of your memories are available for new kinds of learning.

Just a short time ago, you were off track, going sideways and backwards, but now you're totally focused, going steadily forward.

Painful, confusing situations in the past are now a source of insight and new skills. You've always wanted to escape from your past, but now, everything you've experienced since your earliest days is suddenly useful to your thinking of a bigger, better future.

Lights off, lights on.
Suddenly, you can see more clearly, and you're amazed at how deep and wide your new sense of attention goes.

This is the first time you've become aware that your attention is your property—the first time you're aware that this is a fundamental capability you can keep expanding for the rest of your life.

This is the moment of truth. You're now recognizing that no one has the right to tell you what to do with your attention. You're the only one who has ownership of it, and no one else even needs to know what you're choosing to focus your attention on.

Before, you didn't question whether you had power over what you were paying attention to or if it was the other way around. Now you know that you're only really being attentive if you have power over your interpretation of what's happening to you. You're the one who gives meaning to your experiences. On the other hand, if what you're paying attention to has the power, you're not really being attentive.

Huge jump in learning.

When you're controlling your attention, you're learning. It's remarkable when you think about it: in spite of all the months and years in the past when you allowed other people, things, and situations to distract you, you nevertheless learned a lot. Now, with full, conscious attention, you'll learn massively more.

You now have the capability to go back through all of your life experiences and take from them what's useful to you now. Even though many experiences were painful at the time, you now know that they were only negative because you weren't controlling your attention. And that won't happen again.

Now that you're conscious, you can reinterpret every single experience from your past. You can finally eliminate the feelings of sadness, anger, frustration, and failure, and turn every experience into a learning experience.

Suddenly valuable past.

There's a fundamental and fast re-evaluation of what your past now means to you. It's way more valuable and useful to you than it once seemed.

Yesterday, so many of your past experiences seemed like a waste. Now, every time you focus your attention on any memory, that situation takes on new meaning.

You hadn't yet realized that your attention was your property, and so you weren't fully conscious during past experiences. But now you completely control your attention, and you can learn from past situations by looking at them from a perspective you didn't have back then.

For any situation in your life where you had an intense experience but weren't truly conscious, you can now review that situation from the standpoint of how it would have gone had you been conscious, as you are now. You can forgive yourself for what you didn't know before and see every past situation with this new focus, through this new lens.

Marvelously multiplying future.

When you see entirely new meaning in your past, this realization multiplies your confidence about your future. For the first time in your life, you're convinced that it's your unique sense of attention to what you've already experienced that creates your future.

If an experience is negative every time you think about it, it's going to continue to be negative in the future. So, right off the bat, part of your future is being used up with past experiences you find negative.

It's not very motivating, and it can make you not want to be conscious during future experiences.

Now that you've reclaimed your property and eliminated distractions, you have the ability to clean up your past so it contains no disincentives to being conscious during future experiences.

Nothing's wasted or lost.

Any regrets you've had up until now are quickly melting away. With a sense of complete ownership of your personal attention now working in your favor, you know that you're creating an abundant future.

You attach meaning to your own experiences. You have the power to decide in the present what you want every past experience to mean. This is what taking ownership of your attention—which is your property—means for you.

There is nothing that's happened to you that's a failure or mistake. Everything is a capability.

You can go back and examine any negative experience you've had in the past, and while you still might not like how it went, you can give it meaning that's relevant and useful to you now.

PAST
BIGGER
BIGGER
BIGGER
BIGGER
BIGGER
BA
MEANING
VALUE
USEFULNESS
INSIGHT
LEARNING
TRANSFORMATION

Chapter 8
Your 100% Keeps Expanding
You're thrilled to get back more attention than you believe you lost, and then your ownership keeps multiplying.

Suddenly gaining full control over your attention fills you with confidence. This is in contrast to the many scary situations when you *weren't* paying attention to what was most important. It's like suddenly realizing that you just crossed a busy street without checking for traffic. You lose confidence just imagining how badly things could have turned out.

On the other hand, perhaps your most enjoyable and meaningful experiences were where you were fully attentive. If it's the case that your confidence about the future is always the result of controlling your attention in the present, then your life is going to continue to be more enjoyable and meaningful. Every day going forward, you can increase the number of times you are confidently attentive.

Attention generates confidence.
Every time you gain control of your attention—that is, you're aware that you're actually alive and in the present—you also feel confident.

And you raise the value of your past experiences by looking at what they mean to you now and making them relevant and useful to your future. If you felt that someone else controlled your experience, then you might think of your experiences as static, but now that you've taken 100 percent ownership of your attention, your experiences are yours, and you can dynamically work with them in any way you want. This raises the level of confidence that you take into new situations.

Along with your growing confidence, you'll become increasingly skilled at eliminating inessential aspects of experiences as you consciously live through them, becoming more effective.

You are fully owning your experience, which means that you can think and plan your best possible activity without any outside interference.

How your future gets better.

Simply by owning who you are in the present, you can immediately visualize a more positive future. You might be surprised that your future has never been some destination outside of yourself, but is simply the result of taking control of your present.

A lot of people find life to be unpredictable because they, themselves, are unpredictable. They don't feel that happiness is under their control.

But you've made things more predictable by making how you *interpret* your experiences predictable. In other words, you know that no matter what happens in the future, you're going to take each experience, extract the negativity, and make it mean something positive moving forward.

You can't control what happens outside of yourself, but you have increasing control over what happens inside of yourself in relationship to external events.

Trigger your attention with existing habits.

You can also use any and all of your existing daily habits to trigger your attention. Every time you perform one of your daily actions, remind yourself to be in the present moment. You already have dozens of activities that you can use to increasingly expand your control of your attention.

Each of your existing habits started out conscious and intentional, but then you repeated it over and over again, and it became unconscious. So what you have to do is zero in on one of these unconscious habits and resolve to be conscious while doing it.

If you brush your teeth twice a day, then say to yourself, "Every time I brush my teeth, I'm going to remember to be present for those two minutes." You can start by being consciously present while brushing your teeth once a day, and the next day, be consciously present both times. The time adds up, and it's time you're getting back in your day.

Awareness is its own reward.

You're immediately rewarded for transforming your first daily habit into an awareness trigger. You can now do this every day for the rest of your life. Your sense of controlling and owning your attention takes a jump because you also know that you can add a second habit, and a third, etc.

When you're fully present, you're experiencing things in ways that are unique to you. You can't compare one person's uniqueness with another's because their experience is on the inside.

I've also noticed that I'm never bothered when I'm fully present, and in that state of awareness, there's a lot of possibility. I'm not jaded, cynical, or resigned—there's just a sense of potential. Nothing's controlling me.

Your expanding 100% self.

No one can actually exist in the past or the future, even for a moment. The past and the future are mental constructs, and we can only ever truly exist in the present.

You now know that your "self" is simply your experience of being consciously aware in the present. When it happens, you experience 100 percent who you actually are.

This is never a negative experience, and you can control when it happens. You don't need anyone else to participate or even for anyone else to understand it.

There are some people who need proof in order to accept something, but when you experience being 100 percent who you are by being fully present and owning your attention, the experience itself is your proof. Whether anyone believes you will have no bearing on the usefulness of the experience for you.

Who you are is 100 percent your property, and your ownership can continually expand. Taking greater and greater ownership of your own experience takes nothing away from anybody else. In fact, your example will inspire others when they see how positive it is for you.

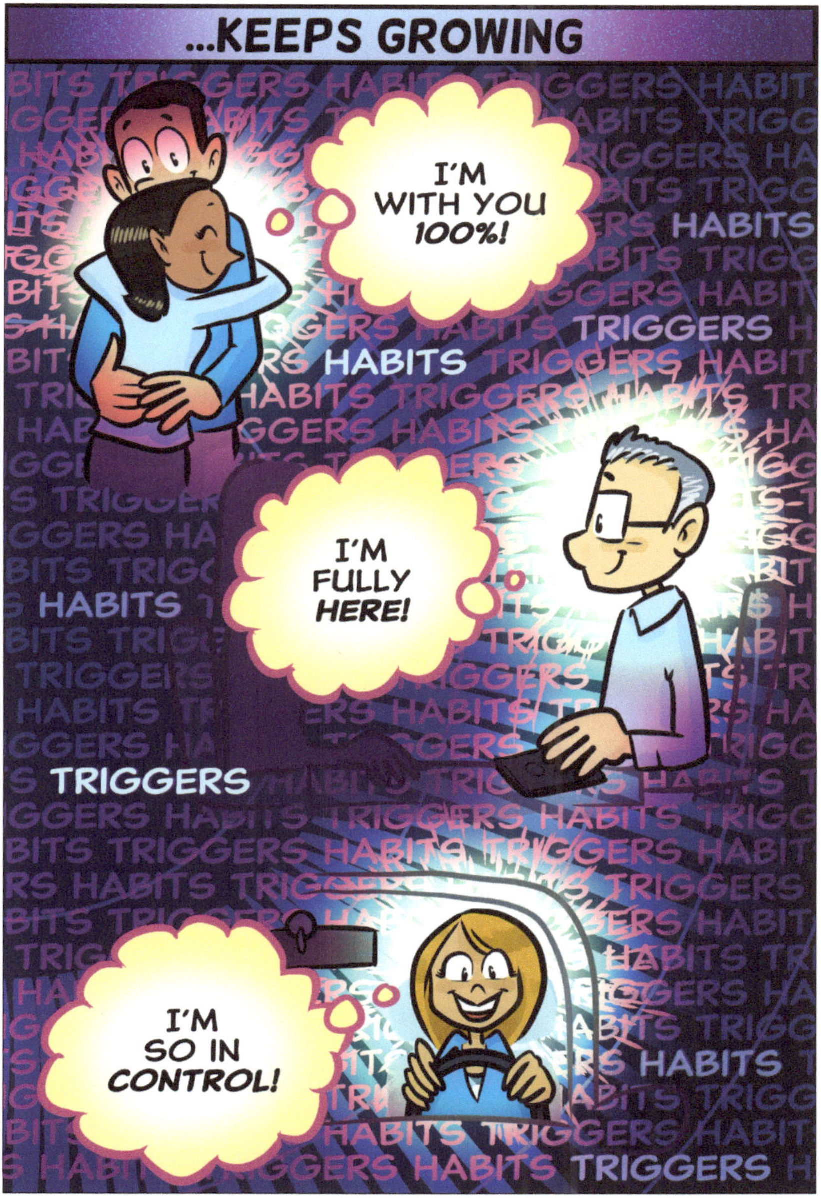
...KEEPS GROWING
I'M WITH YOU 100%!
I'M FULLY HERE!
I'M SO IN CONTROL!

Conclusion

Owning What You've Created

Your lifetime experience becomes uniquely meaningful as you expand your "attention property."

We take what constitutes our property very seriously, but most people don't know that their attention is their property, so they don't look seriously enough at who is controlling their attention. You can't manage your attention until you treat it as your property.

Before now, you probably hadn't connected your experience of *attention* with the concept of *property*. But once you put these two thoughts together, an amazing number of other things become suddenly clear. You realize that you "own" every part of your life: all of your time, all of your situations, and now all of your lessons. They're all yours, because you're the only one who knows what all of these experiences are and what they mean. No one else can have any insights into the life you've led unless you tell them.

Your life belongs to you. It's all reserved for your unique attention, and it's all your exclusive property.

Your whole life connects.

While you've had many different experiences over the course of your life, you're always the same person—you're always uniquely you as long as you're fully in control of your attention. And every part of your life connects with every other part through the uniqueness of your attention.

There's something about being present with your attention that results in a much more powerful memory than if something just happens to you and you weren't truly conscious at the time. In a sense, the past is created through the combination of all the experiences where you were actually present.

Looking back on my life, I realize that who I was as a child is the same person I am now. When you're owning your attention, you're always the same person—that person is who you really are and isn't influenced by what others think about who you are.

Every experience counts.

You might have felt that some of the situations in your life were wasted. But now you've discovered that all of your experiences are significant and meaningful.

They all count when you pay attention to them. And now, when you devote your attention to the "wasted" experiences, they also count for a lot. So, nothing is lost. No matter how you previously thought about a past experience, and no matter how it felt at the time, you can now extract the value of the experience in the present, making it useful to you for your future.

This also allows you to get rid of any kind of negativity that certain memories hold for you. Once you gain the lesson from a memory, you've turned it into something positive. And you now own that experience, not the other way around.

More years, big meaning.

You've heard others talk about how their lives were exciting and interesting when they were younger but that things got boringly the same as they got older. You now understand clearly that it's all a matter of owning your attention.

The clearer this becomes, the more your years and experiences matter. If you develop a habit of increasingly directing and focusing your attention, you get enormous value out of the passage of time.

You'll recognize better than most that you should be focusing only on applying your best abilities to each situation. You'll eliminate everything else from your mind, recognizing that it's all a distraction. You'll gain an implicit understanding of what's required in new situations early on. And your teamwork and leadership capabilities will improve.

Willing to be wonderfully wise.

The more you own your attention, the wiser you get. This is because you only really get the benefit of those experiences you pay attention to and claim as your exclusive property. The moment you're willing to learn deeply from more of your experiences, the wiser you become.

If you fully believe in something, would it make any difference whatsoever if you were the only one who believed in it? When I ask people this question, it often throws them for a loop because they associate their own meaning with persuading other people to accept their meaning.

But this doesn't have to be the case. You have enormous wisdom because you're not asking other people to see things the way you see them. What you're asking other people to do is to see things the way *they* see them.

You want to know how other people see things because that allows you to add that dimension to your understanding. You're interested in being influenced by other people, but you don't need them to be influenced by you. If you weren't wise, if you weren't certain about your beliefs, you would be trying to persuade others to think the way you do, and you'd be bothered if they didn't.

Making it completely yours.

You know from study, observation, and discussion that many people feel that their lives passed them by while they were paying attention to other things. What was happening outside of them was always more important than what was happening inside.

But that's not you. You own your attention. It's completely your property. Only you decide what to focus your attention on, and you won't be tricked into allowing your attention to be used for other people's purposes instead of your own. You're free from manipulation.

You're also the only one who controls what meaning all of your experiences have, and you can transform any experience to extract the value from it and eliminate any negatives, all while you grant the same freedoms to everyone else.

No one else can tell you what or how to feel about something or what difference it makes to you. You completely own that. It's yours. And with this newfound recognition that your attention is your property, you'll find yourself feeling less fear and greater confidence, and you'll be more present in your everyday life.

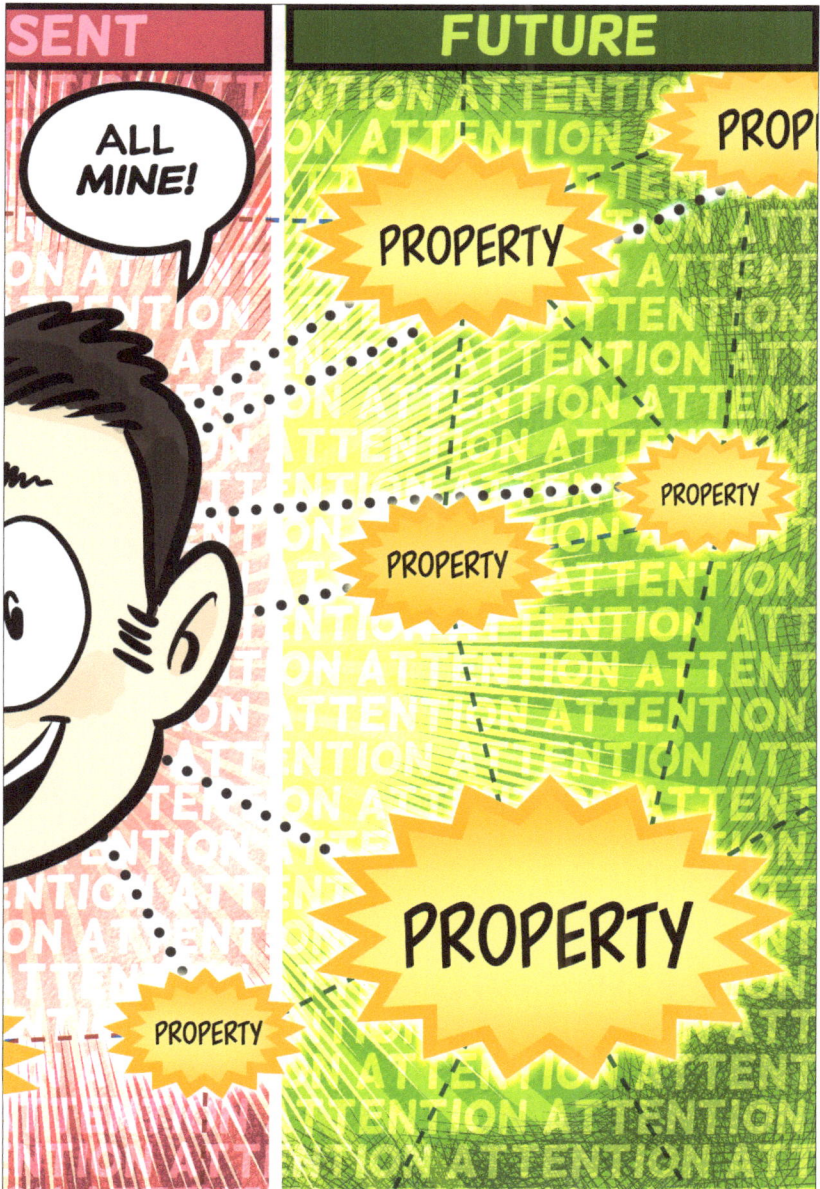

The Strategic Coach Program
For Ambitious, Collaborative Entrepreneurs
You commit to growing upward through three transformative levels, giving yourself 25 years to exponentially improve every aspect of your work and life.

"Your Attention: Your Property" is a crucial capability and a natural result of everything we coach in The Strategic Coach Program, a quarterly workshop experience for successful entrepreneurs who are committed and devoted to business and industry transformation for the long-term, for 25 years and beyond.

The Program has a destination for all participants—creating more and more of what we call "Free Zone Frontiers." This means taking advantage of your own unique capabilities, the unique capabilities around you, your unique opportunities, and your unique circumstances, and putting the emphasis on creating a life that is free of competition.

Most entrepreneurs grow up in a system where they think competition is the name of the game. The general way of looking at the world is that the natural state of affairs is competition, and collaboration is an anomaly.

Free Zone Frontier
The Free Zone Frontier is a whole new level of entrepreneurship that many people don't even know is possible. But once you start putting the framework in place, new

possibilities open up for you. You create zones that are purely about collaboration. You start recognizing that collaboration is the natural state, and competition is the anomaly. It makes you look at things totally differently.

Strategic Coach has continually created concepts and thinking tools that allow entrepreneurs to more and more see their future in terms of Free Zones that have no competition.

Three levels of entrepreneurial growth.

Strategic Coach participants continually transform how they think, make decisions, communicate, and take action based on their use of dozens of unique entrepreneurial mindsets we've developed. The Program has been refined through decades of entrepreneurial testing and is the most concentrated, massive discovery process in the world created solely for transformative entrepreneurs who want to create new Free Zones.

Over the years, we've observed that our clients' development happens in levels of mastery. And so, we've organized the Program into three levels of participation, each of which involves two different types of transformation:

The Signature Level. The first level is devoted to your *personal* transformation, which has to do with how you're spending your time as an entrepreneur as well as how you're taking advantage of your personal freedom outside of business that your entrepreneurial success affords you. Focusing on improving yourself on a personal level before you move on to making significant changes in other aspects of your life and business is key because you have to simplify before you can multiply.

The second aspect of the Signature Level is how you look at your *teamwork*. This means seeing that your future consists of teamwork with others whose unique capabilities complement your own, leading to bigger and better goals that constantly get achieved at a measurably higher rate.

The 10x Ambition Level. Once you feel confident about your own personal transformation and have access to ever-expanding teamwork, you can think much bigger in terms of your *company*. An idea that at one time would have seemed scary and even impossible—growing your business 10x—is no longer a wild dream but a result of the systematic expansion of the teamwork model you've established. And because you're stable in the center, you won't get thrown off balance by exponential growth. Your life stays balanced and integrated even as things grow around you.

And that's when you're in a position to transform your relationship with your *market*. This is when your company has a huge impact on the marketplace that competitors can't even understand because they're not going through this transformative structure or thinking in terms of 25 years as you are. Thinking in terms of 25 years gives you an expansive sense of freedom and the ability to have big picture goals.

The Free Zone Frontier Level. Once you've mastered the first four areas of transformation, you're at the point where your company is self-managing and self-multiplying, which means that your time can now be totally freed up. At this stage, competitors become collaborators and it becomes all about your *industry*. You can consider everything you've created as a single capability you can now match up with another company's to create collaborations that go way beyond 10x.

And, finally, it becomes *global*. You immediately see that there are possibilities of going global—it's just a matter of combining your capabilities with those of others to create something exponentially bigger than you could ever have achieved on your own.

Global collaborative community.

Entrepreneurism can be a lonely activity. You have goals that the people you grew up with don't understand. Your family might not comprehend you at all and don't know why you keep wanting to expand, why you want to take new risks, why you want to jump to the next level. And so it becomes proportionately more important as you gain your own individual mastery that you're in a community of thousands of individuals who are on exactly the same journey.

In The Strategic Coach Program, you benefit from not only your own continual individual mastery but from the constant expansion of support from and collaboration with a growing global community of extraordinarily liberated entrepreneurs who will increasingly share with you their deep wisdom and creative breakthroughs as innovators in hundreds of different industries and markets.

If you've reached a jumping off point in your entrepreneurial career where you're beyond ready to multiply all of your capabilities and opportunities into a 10x more creative and productive formula that keeps getting simpler and more satisfying, we're ready for you.

For more information and to register for The Strategic Coach Program, call 416.531.7399 or 1.800.387.3206, or visit us online at *strategiccoach.com*.

THREE LEVELS OF

FREE ZONE FRONTIER

- 100x Collaboration
- Perfect Fit VISION
- 25-Year Hero Target
- 100% Simplifier/Multiplier
- $15-Trillion Free Zone

10X AMBITION

- Self-Multiplying Company
- Simplifier/Multiplier
- Total Cash Confidence
- Always Be The Buyer
- The D.O.S. Conversation

SIGNATURE

- Self-Managing Company
- The Lifetime Extender
- Free, Focus, and Buffer Days
- Unique Ability Teamwork
- The Largest Cheque

FREE ZONE

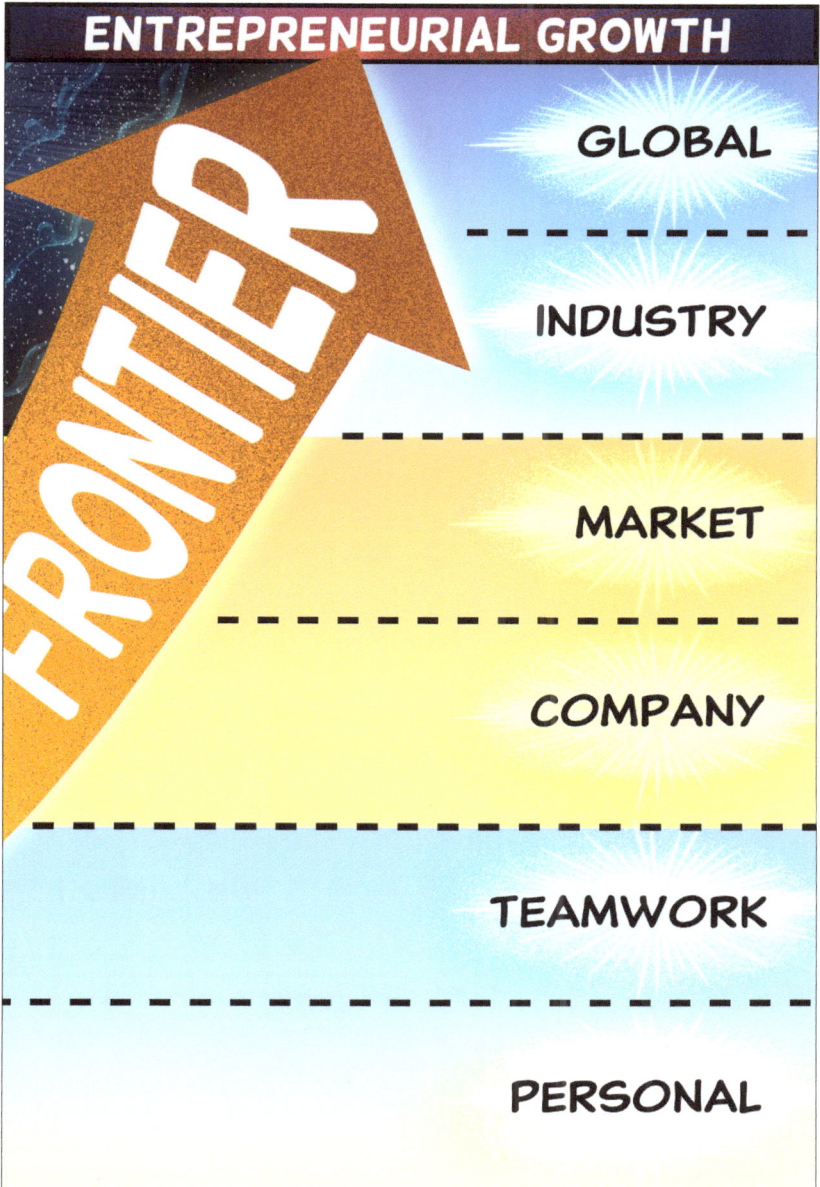

ENTREPRENEURIAL GROWTH

FRONTIER

GLOBAL

INDUSTRY

MARKET

COMPANY

TEAMWORK

PERSONAL

Your Attention: Your Property Scorecard

Fold out this Mindset Scorecard and read through the four statements for each mindset. Give yourself a score of 1 to 12 based on where your own mindset falls on the spectrum. Put each mindset's score in the first column at the right, and then add up all eight and put the total at the bottom.

Then, think about what scores would represent progress for you over the next quarter. Write these in the second scoring column, add them up, and write in the total.

When you compare the two scores, you can see where you want to go in terms of your achievements and ambitions.

Mindsets	1	2	3	4	5	6
1 **You Know That Feeling**	You've never experienced being present with yourself, where you felt safe and in control of who you were. Instead, you always feel controlled by events.			You've recently had experiences that made you realize you're wasting too much of your attention on things that don't benefit you at all.		
2 **Where You've Been Rewarded**	You've always been distracted by what other people are doing. Nothing you're doing is as important to you as what others are doing.			You've tried to pay attention to what the most successful people are doing, but now you need to pay increasing attention to what you're successfully doing.		
3 **When Others Own Your Attention**	You've always been in an anxious state because nothing has ever come easily for you. No matter what you've wanted to achieve, you've always been frustrated.			You realize that almost everything in your life that frustrates you is also where you've allowed other people and things to control your attention.		
4 **How You Lose Attention**	You've always seen your own experiences as worthless and meaningless when compared to what others are doing.			You're increasingly clear that your own experiences have far more to teach you than trying to duplicate other people's experiences.		
5 **Getting It All Back**	You feel increasingly that you've wasted your life, never focusing on anything worthwhile, and now it's too late for anything to get better.			You now know that not controlling your own attention wastes your energy and undermines your confidence, so you're committed to regaining control.		
6 **Courage Is Capability**	You see yourself as victimized by everything that's ever happened to you. The notion that you could ever be in control of your life seems ridiculous.			You know from past experiences that improving any capability requires a period of courage before things get better. That's where you are now.		
7 **Incredibly Fast Progress**	You realize that you've given up on ever being someone you can feel proud of. Past, present, or future, there'll never be anything you do that's worthwhile.			You're just starting on this new path, and it's actually shocking how bad it feels to do any of the activities where you've been wasting your attention.		
8 **Your 100% Keeps Expanding**	You're convinced that you never had a chance to be confident and capable, especially now that there's no possibility of turning things around.			You suspect it might be possible that all the ways of being "owned" by other people and things are going away. It's almost too good to be true.		
Scorecard	➡	➡	➡	➡	➡	➡	➡	➡

7	8	9	10	11	12	Score Now	Score Next
You've created a successful life by always paying attention to what more successful people told you was important to them. You follow what they do.			You have great memories of situations where you felt totally in control of your attention, when you were completely focused on your own unique purpose.				
Your progress and success in both your work and personal life have come from paying careful attention to everyone who can promote you higher.			You can see that your biggest progress, achievement, and success have come from fully focusing your attention.				
You realized very early in your life, from your parents and teachers, that your individual status comes from paying attention to who has the most status.			You realize that all of your anxieties and frustrations distract you when you allow others to control your attention.				
You've always known that your own experience is only important to the degree that it's inside of the experience of smarter and more talented people.			You realize that you lose control of your own attention when you think others' experiences are more important than yours.				
Your biggest goal right now is to protect your reputation for having paid attention to being popular within the right groups in every area of your life.			You're relieved and happy that all of your lost attention starts coming back to you the moment you choose to take ownership of it.				
You're accepting that you were fortunate to have paid attention to the best opportunities in the past, because you're no longer capable of that now.			You are committed to taking back all of your attention — and your courage to do this provides 100% ownership.				
You're increasingly nostalgic about the times when you and your current friends were devoting your best attention to exciting, energizing goals.			You are amazed that decades of giving away your attention can be completely reversed in a remarkably short time.				
You can tell that time is speeding up and you're slowing down. So much of your attention is now given over to past events you wish you could do again.			You're thrilled to get back more attention than you believe you lost, and then your ownership keeps multiplying.				

79

About The Author
Dan Sullivan

Dan Sullivan is the founder and president of The Strategic Coach Inc. and creator of The Strategic Coach® Program, which helps accomplished entrepreneurs reach new heights of success and happiness. He is author of over 50 publications, including *The Great Crossover, The 21st Century Agent, Creative Destruction, How The Best Get Better*, and The Ambition Series of quarterly small books. He is co-author of *Who Not How, The Laws of Lifetime Growth*, and *The Advisor Century*.